The Moon Was There

Glimpses from the Báb's Childhood for Young Children

Written by Alhan Rahimi
Illustrations by Anahit Aleksanyan

Copyright © 2019, 2021 by Alhan Rahimi
alhan@persianarabic.com

ISBN: 978-1-694182-87-6 (paperback)
ISBN: 978-1-990286-04-9 (hardcover)

Written by Alhan Rahimi based on true historical events

Illustrations and cover design by Anahit Aleksanyan

All rights reserved worldwide. No part of this book may be reproduced, distributed or transmitted in any form or by any means without the prior written permission of the author, except in the case of brief quotations.

This book has been approved by the National Spiritual Assembly of the Bahá'ís of Canada.

Hello, my friends.

I am the Moon—yes, the same moon you can see most nights in the sky.

I have been here
for a very long time.
I have seen many things.

Today, I want to tell
you a story about a very
special Child.

This story happened
in a place called Persia.
This place could be very far
away from you.

I marked it in red on the map.
Can you find where you
are on the map?

This young Child was born before dawn, shortly before I disappeared and my friend, the sun, came out.

The Child's family was very happy about His birth. He was their only Child.

I was very excited, and even the stars were blinking and smiling!

The birds were singing after they had just woken up. Everyone and everything was happy.

The Child's family named Him Siyyid `Alí Muḥammad, and He later became known as

THE BÁB.

The Báb means the Gate in Arabic. He was the Gate to a new message from God.

He was an extraordinary child.
That means He was different
from other children who were
the same age.

He loved praying and He prayed
with such a beautiful voice.

I will tell you one story that
will explain how different
He was from other children.

Every week, the Báb's teacher took the students to a park to play.

While everyone was playing, the teacher realized that the Báb was missing!

Everybody started searching until they finally found Him. Can you guess where He was and what He was doing?

He was under the shade of some trees, praying! He liked praying more than playing.

His teacher loved Him very much
and was always amazed by Him.
He knew the Báb had something
special that no other student
had. He was right.

When the Báb grew up,
He had a very important message
from God to all people.
His teacher listened to Him and
His message, just like many others did.

Some of the things that
the Báb liked to do as a child
were praying, studying
and writing.

He was always kind,
loving and generous
to other children.

For example, He would give
away any food He brought
with Him to His classmates
at school.

Today, millions of people
all over the world celebrate
His birthday.

How do you celebrate it?

Room where the Báb was born, Shíráz

The Báb's prayer beads

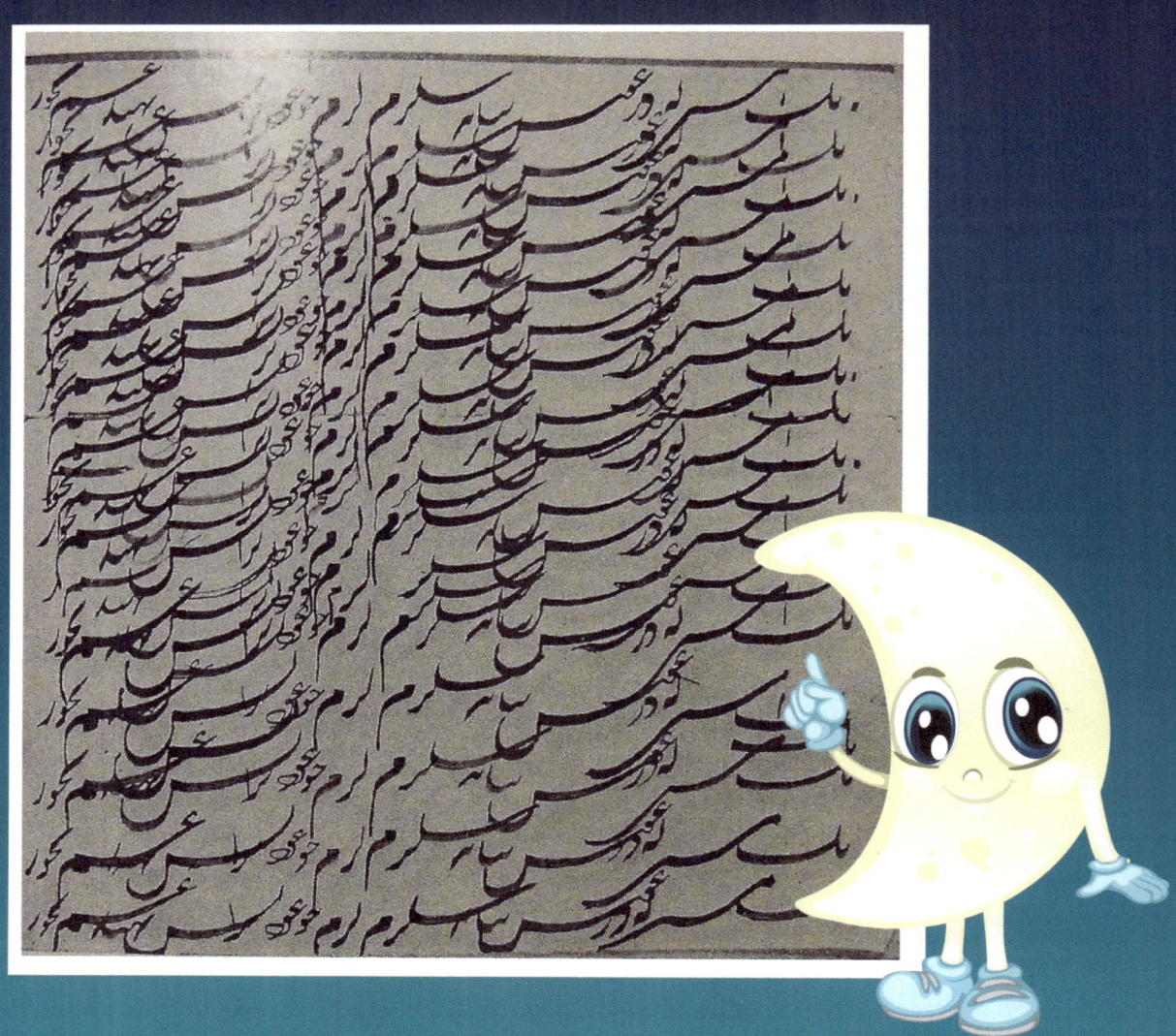

Calligraphic exercise of the Báb written before He was ten years old

View of the front door of the House of the Báb, S͟híráz

Overview of the House of the Báb, Shíráz

Orange tree planted by the Báb in the courtyard of His house, Shíráz

Shrine of the Báb and surrounding gardens

References:

1. The Báb, by Balyuzi, H.M.
2. The Báb, His Life, His Writings And The Disciples Of The Báb's Dispensation, by Nusrat'u'lláh Muhammad-Husainí, Ph.D.
3. Ḥaḍrat-i-Nuqṭay-i Úlá, The Life Of The Báb, by Muḥammad-`Alí Fayḍí
4. https://media.bahai.org/

www.ingramcontent.com/pod-product-compliance
Lightning Source LLC
Chambersburg PA
CBHW040758240426
43673CB00014B/379